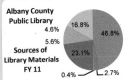

FROGS!

STRANGE AND WONDERFUL

Laurence Pringle

Illustrated by Meryl Henderson

BOYDS MILLS PRESS

HONESDALE, PENNSYLVANIA

To Lena Korman-Keyes
Like a chorus of spring peepers, Lena is full of life, hope,
and a promise of many good things to come.
                              —LP

To Grace
You are the best stepmother ever!
                              —MH

The author wishes to thank Marty Crump, PhD, adjunct professor, Department of Biological Sciences, Northern Arizona University, and Rafe M. Brown, PhD, curator in charge of herpetology at the KU Natural History Museum and associate professor, Department of Ecology and Evolutionary Biology, University of Kansas, for their thorough review of the manuscript and illustrations.

Boyds Mills Press, Inc.
815 Church Street
Honesdale, Pennsylvania 18431
Printed in China

ISBN: 978-1-59078-371-9
Library of Congress Control Number: 2011928834

The text of this book is set in 13-point ITC Clearface.
The illustrations are done in watercolor.

10 9 8 7 6 5 4 3 2 1

Make a sound like a frog.

Go ahead. Pretend you are a frog, and make its sound.

Did you make a croaking noise? Or did you say, "*ribbit, ribbit, ribbit*"? Good, but that is only a start. You could also say, "*gick, gick, gick*" or "*heck, heck, heck*" or "*wonk, wonk, wonk*" or "*pu-tunk, pu-tunk, pu-tunk.*" There are many kinds of frogs, and they make an amazing variety of sounds.

Some quack like ducks. Some bleat like sheep. Some bark like dogs. Some sound like sleigh bells, others like plucked banjo strings. If you grunt, peep, chirp, trill, whistle, or snore, you sound like some of the more than six thousand kinds of frogs that live on Earth.

Only the Pacific tree frog of the western United States says "ribbit."

Spring peeper

Barking tree frog

Northern red salamander

Hellbender

Mudpuppy

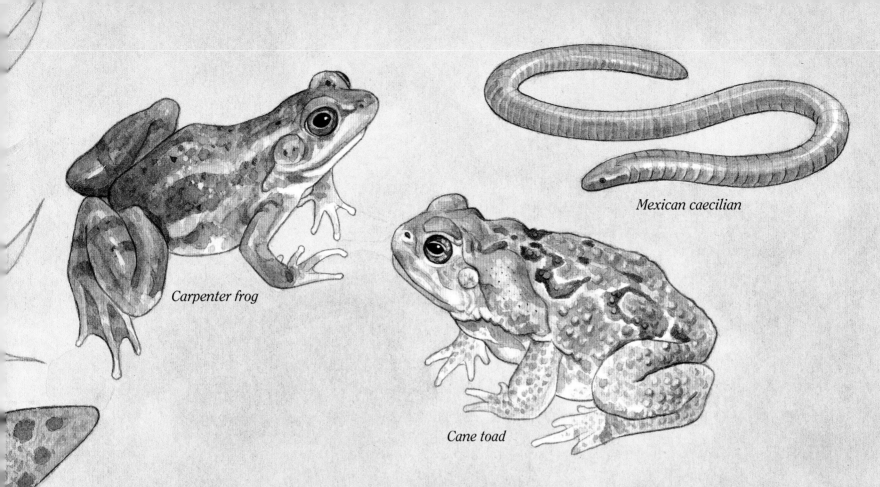

Carpenter frog

Mexican caecilian

Cane toad

Frogs live just about everywhere, including southern parts of the Arctic (but not in Antarctica). They belong to a group of animals called amphibians. Salamanders are also amphibians, and so are caecilians (which are legless and live mostly in the tropics).

The word amphibian means "double life" or "two lives." Most amphibians start their lives in the water and breathe underwater through gills. As adults, most live on land and breathe through lungs. This is true of amphibians in general, but there are lots of exceptions, including frogs, salamanders, and caecilians that never get into water and others that never leave water. In North America, some water-dwelling salamanders have unusual names: mudpuppy, waterdog, and hellbender!

Scientists who study frogs are called herpetologists. When they speak or write about these animals they usually call them anurans, because they are all classified in a group, the order Anura (which means "without tail"). Anurans are alike in some important ways. Their rear legs are longer than their front legs. Most have big, bulgy eyes. Also, most have lungs but can also breathe through their skin. Amphibians called toads are frogs, too. Toads tend to have drier, bumpier skin and shorter legs than other frogs have.

TRUE FROGS

American bullfrog *Carpenter frog*

TRUE TOADS

American green toad *Southern toad*

SPADEFOOT TOADS

Common spadefoot *Couch's spadefoot*

AUSTRALIAN GROUND FROGS

Crucifix frog *Turtle frog*

SOUTHERN FROGS

Lake Titicaca frog *Ornate horned frog*

ASIAN TOADFROGS

Malayan horned frog *Asian leaf frog*

TREE FROGS

White's tree frog

Red-eyed tree frog

GLASS FROGS

La Palma glass frog

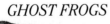

Bare-hearted glass frog

GHOST FROGS

Natal ghost frog

Cape ghost frog

TONGUELESS FROGS

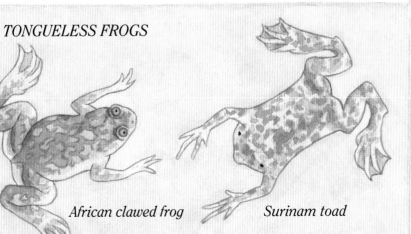

African clawed frog

Surinam toad

POISON FROGS

Harlequin poison frog

Green-and-black poison frog

PURPLE FROG

Purple burrowing frog

SHOVEL-NOSED FROGS

Shovel-nosed frog

Spotted shovel-nosed frog

NARROW-MOUTHED FROGS

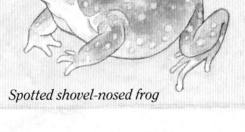

Great Plains
narrow-mouthed toad

Tomato frog

7

Herpetologists rarely say, "All frogs do this," or "All frogs have that." These animals are just too varied, too amazingly different. Just as they make many different kinds of sounds, they differ greatly in size, in color, in their ways of mating and producing young, and in the ways they live.

For example, if you draw a frog, you do not draw a tail. Remember, the order of frogs is Anura—Greek for "no tail." This is true for more than six thousand species, but not for the tailed frog that lives in cold mountain streams in northwestern North America. Or you might think that all anurans move by leaping or hopping. Their long hind legs help them do this. Also, after a jump, their strong shoulder bones absorb the shock of landing. However, the Senegal running frog is named for its unusual way of moving. And in Asia several kinds of frogs can travel by "flying." When they spread the webbing between the toes of all four feet, they can glide from one tree to another, or from a tree to the ground.

Leopard frog

Among the greatest leapers are the leopard frog, which can jump 15 times its body length, and the southern cricket frog, which can leap 36 times its body length.

Reinwardt's flying frog

Tailed frog

Senegal running frog

Goliath frog

African bullfrog

Some frogs are so big that you need two hands to hold them. Others are so tiny that they can perch on your fingernail. Big frogs can easily gobble down smaller frogs—and they do.

The bullfrog of North America is best known for its deep, loud voice—calling "*rum . . . rum . . . rum*," and sometimes "*jug-o-rum*." The bullfrog sometimes eats smaller frogs, as well as insects, snakes, fishes, and even birds and mice. The biggest frog in North America, it can measure eight inches, nose to end. The giant bullfrog of Africa is about two inches longer and has sharp teeth. When defending its eggs or young, this feisty frog attacks large birds, people, and even lions.

The biggest frog of all is the goliath frog of western Africa. It can grow to be thirteen inches long and weigh more than six pounds.

One of Earth's smallest frogs was discovered in Cuba in 1993. It can perch its whole body on a United States dime. The Brazilian gold frog is equally tiny. These frogs are tied for the title of "world's smallest four-footed animal."

American bullfrog

Gold frog

Cuban frog

To catch food and escape enemies, frogs need good eyesight. The bulging eyes of many anurans can see in front, above, to the sides, and even behind their heads. Their eyes are especially good at sensing movement. The iris (colored part) of anuran eyes can be red, orange, yellow, blue, green, brown, bronze, gold, or silver. Frogs also have different shapes of pupils (the opening at the center of the eyes). Pupils can be round, heart-shaped, diamond-shaped, horizontal, or vertical. Vertical pupils—"cat eyes"—are especially good for night vision. Frogs with this pupil shape usually hunt at night.

When a frog grabs food in its mouth, it blinks. Muscles pull the eyeballs down into the head and press them against the roof of the mouth. This helps push the food down the frog's throat.

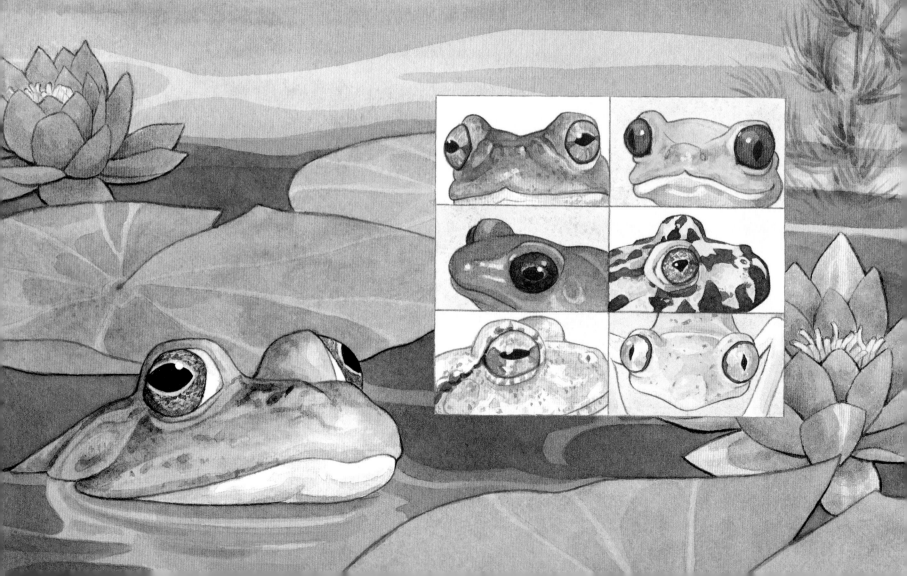

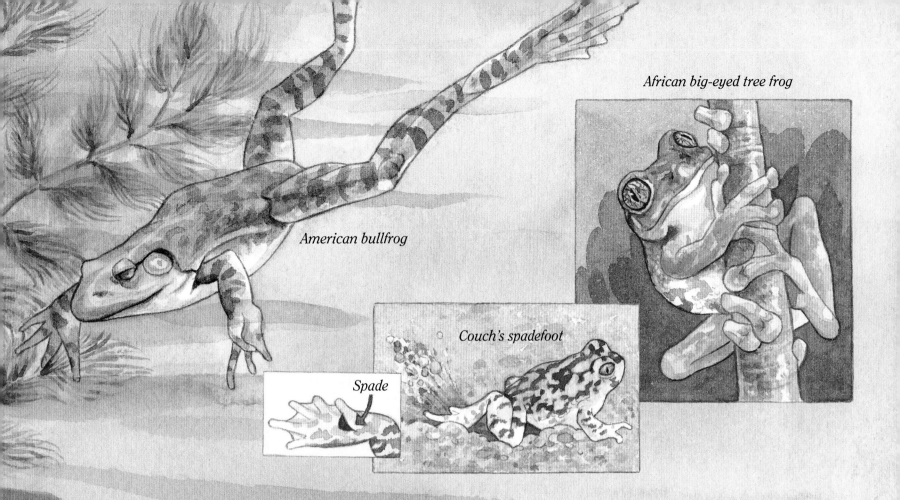

African big-eyed tree frog

American bullfrog

Couch's spadefoot

Spade

You can learn a lot about a frog's life by looking at its feet. If there is webbing between the toes of its hind feet, it swims well. If it has a hard claw-like growth on each hind foot, it is probably a spadefoot toad. It digs into sand or soft soil with this "spade" (a kind of shovel) to burrow underground. It rests there during long dry periods. Other anurans, including the banjo frog of Australia and the giant bullfrog of Africa, also have "spades" on their hind feet for digging.

If a frog has sticky pads on all of its long fingers and toes, it is a good climber. It is probably a tree frog. On each toe pad, tiny interlocking cells grip the surface and enable a tree frog to climb any surface, even glass.

13

Frogs eat just about any animal they can gulp down. At least one kind of anuran eats plants, and some small species hop along the forest floor, looking for insects, but most are sit-and-wait predators. They stay still and watch for something on the move.

A frog's tongue is attached to the front of its lower jaw. (Yours is attached at the back of your mouth.) It lies folded on the floor of the mouth and has a sticky tip. When a frog tries to grab an insect, the tongue flicks out. In an instant, the insect is stuck to the tongue, and the tongue folds back into the frog's mouth. Gulp!

American toad

Some frogs are masters of camouflage. The colors and patterns on their skins help them hide from enemies. Camouflage also helps them surprise animals they can catch and eat.

Tree frogs are often colored green. They are hard to see as they clamber on stems and leaves of trees and other plants. The gray tree frog can change color. On tree bark it can be gray; surrounded by living plants, it can be green.

Some anurans are also shaped in ways that help them blend in among dead leaves, mosses, or other plants on the forest floor. One of the most hard-to-see anurans is the ornate horned frog of South America. It is one of eight species of frogs hidden on these pages. See if you can find it and also a gray tree frog, Solomon Island leaf frog, Vietnamese mossy frog, canyon tree frog, Chinese microhylid, Amazon horned frog, and red-eyed tree frog.

(You can find the answers on page 32.)

Most frogs are well hidden, but some have brightly colored skin that seems to say, "Hey, look at me!" In Madagascar these frogs are called mantellas. In South America and Central America they are called poison frogs.

There are nearly 170 species of poison frogs. To people, their bold colors and patterns gleam like beautiful jewels. However, to snakes, birds, and other animals that sometimes eat frogs, their colors are a warning. Glands in their skin produce poisons (toxins) that can make a predator sick or even kill it. The poisons taste bad, so predators usually let poison frogs go. They learn to avoid them.

To most herpetologists, only three species of poison frogs are called poison dart frogs. The golden poison dart frog of Colombia contains enough toxin to kill ten people or 20,000 mice. Its poison, and that from two related frogs, has been used by the Choco people of Colombia to poison the tips of darts used for hunting mammals and birds. These frogs seem to produce some toxin within their bodies, but other kinds of poison frogs get toxins from the food they eat. Ants they eat in the wild contain poisons called alkaloids. When captive frogs are fed crickets and flies, but no ants, they are no longer poisonous.

Golden mantella

Painted mantella

Ornate mantella

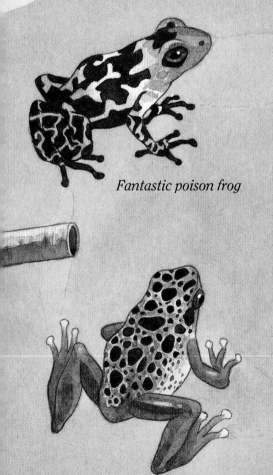

Fantastic poison frog

Strawberry poison frog

Auratus poison frog

Golden poison dart frog

Blue poison frog

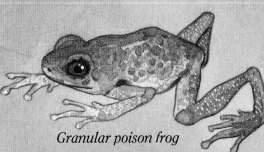

Granular poison frog

Dyeing poison frog

Coqui frog

Green tree frog

When you walk along the shore of a pond or creek, some frogs give a yelp or squeak of alarm as they leap into the water. Most of the time, however, anurans are quiet. Then, at mating time, the males make their special sounds, a sort of frog love song. The mating calls of male frogs say, "Pick me!" to females. Males often have another call that tells other males to stay away. Coqui (ko-KEE) frogs of Puerto Rico do this with one call. *Co* warns other males. *Qui* attracts females.

Frogs keep their mouths closed when they give their mating calls. They breathe air into their lungs through their nostrils. Then muscles squeeze the lungs, forcing air back and forth across their vocal cords and into one or two sacs of loose skin. The frog's voice comes from vibrating vocal cords that send sound waves out from its head in all directions. The loose sacs of skin are called vocal sacs. These sacs help recycle the expelled air, saving energy for frogs during the great effort of calling to attract females. Some frogs have one vocal sac under their chins. Others have a pair of vocal sacs, one on each side.

Some frogs mate near mountain streams where the flowing water is very noisy and may drown out their calls. The males have to get the attention of females in other ways, such as hopping around and waving!

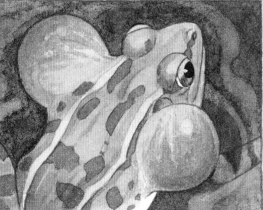

Carpenter frog

American toad

Southern leopard frog

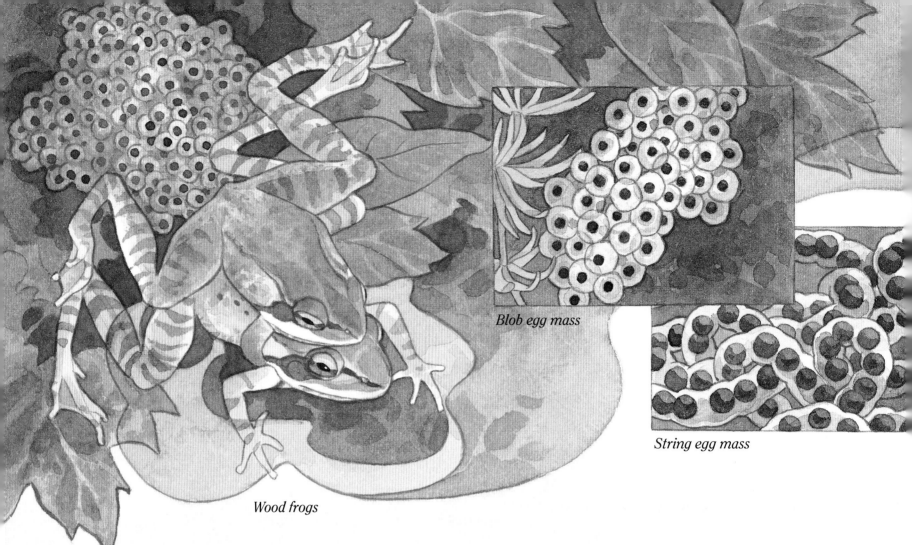

Blob egg mass

String egg mass

Wood frogs

Many kinds of anurans mate in a pond, swamp, or other wetland. Females release eggs into the water, and males fertilize them. Clusters or strings of eggs lie in the water, and the parents leave them unprotected. Within each egg, a yolk provides food for a tiny creature that grows a little bit bigger each day. After hatching, it is called a tadpole or pollywog.

A tadpole looks like a little fish. It has no legs, and moves through the water by swinging its finned tail in the water—as fish do.

Mimic poison frog

Tadpoles filter tiny plants from the water around them or graze on algae and other plant material. As they grow in size, they go through amazing changes. Limb buds sprout from their bodies and develop into legs. The simple tadpole mouth changes into one with jaws and a tongue. The tail gradually shrinks and vanishes. And within each tadpole, lungs develop so the new young frog can breathe oxygen from the air.

In some species, the process takes only a month, in others, more than a year.

Tadpoles of one South American frog grow to be 10 inches long, yet the adults are only 3 inches long. The frog is called the paradoxical frog because its growth pattern is not what you would expect. It's a paradox.

Actual size

Not all frogs mate in the water and leave their eggs there unguarded. Female golden coqui frogs keep their eggs within their bodies and give birth to live young. Other species carry around fertilized eggs, or tadpoles, on their bodies—or inside their bodies. And some frogs stay with their eggs or tadpoles, guarding them against predators.

In the tropics, many frogs lay eggs in wet places on the forest floor. After mating, the male Darwin's frog of South America guards the eggs. When the tadpoles begin to move inside their eggs, the male puts them in his mouth, then into his vocal sac. After about fifty days the tadpoles have become little frogs, ready to live on their own. They hop out of their father's mouth.

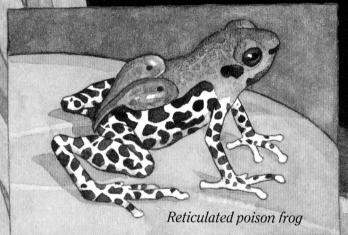

Reticulated poison frog

Male Darwin's frog with young

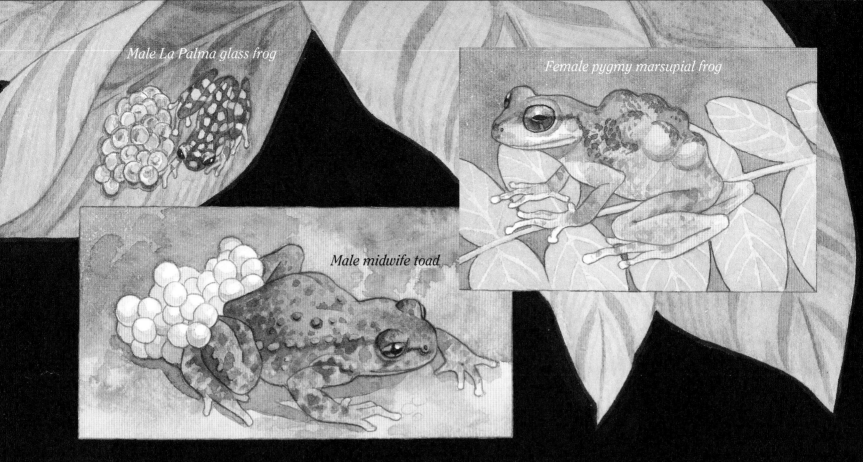

Male La Palma glass frog

Female pygmy marsupial frog

Male midwife toad

Male glass frogs also guard eggs, after they have been laid and fertilized on the underside of a leaf that overhangs a stream. Tadpoles will not develop if the eggs dry out, so sometimes the father pees on them. (The urine may also help protect against an egg-killing fungus.) When the tadpoles hatch, they drop from the leaf into the stream, where they develop into frogs.

Female marsupial frogs of South America carry their fertilized eggs in a pouch on their back until tadpoles hatch from the eggs. In Australia, the males of another species of marsupial frog carry tadpoles in pockets on their hips. And male midwife toads of Europe carry strings of thirty-five to fifty eggs wrapped around their rear legs. When the tadpoles are about ready to hatch from the eggs, the father gets into water. Soon the tadpoles swim away.

The champion anuran egg-layer is the cane toad (sometimes called the marine toad). In one year a female cane toad can lay 35,000 eggs. Tadpoles hatch from the eggs in just a few days. These toads can hop a mile in one night and have overrun large parts of Australia since they were brought there in 1935.

In their native habitats in Central America and South America, cane toads help control insect pests. They were brought to northeastern Australia to eat beetles that damage sugar cane plants. Instead, they eat Australian frogs, honeybees, birds, and many other animals. Cane toads are now a costly nuisance because they were brought to a place where they have no natural enemies. In fact, poisons on their skin kill snakes, lizards, and dogs that attack them. People cannot eat them, which is too bad because killing them for food would help reduce the huge cane toad population.

Cane toads

Edible frog

Mountain chicken

Tricolor poison frog

People do eat anurans. One variety in Europe is called the edible frog. Another kind of big frog that lives on the islands of Dominica and Montserrat in the West Indies is called the mountain chicken. The United States imports over a million pounds of frog legs from Asia each year. Large frogs have been wiped out in many areas. In India and Bangladesh, loss of frogs led to an increase in mosquitoes and in malaria (a disease spread by mosquitoes). The governments of these nations have tried to ban exports of frog legs.

Research on frogs has helped scientists develop helpful medical drugs for people. One toxin from the skin of the tricolor poison frog of Ecuador was found to be two hundred times more effective than morphine as a painkiller. (Morphine is a drug now used to treat intense pain.) The toxin itself is too dangerous to use on humans, but chemists developed a similar medicine that is now being tested. People may someday thank a frog for a drug that helps ease their pain.

The greatest value of anurans is simply being part of nature. Frogs eat countless numbers of insects. Eggs, tadpoles, and adult frogs are eaten by birds, snakes, turtles, raccoons, otters, and many other animals. As prey, and as predators, frogs play key roles in many food webs.

Beginning in the 1980s, scientists and other people became concerned about frogs. There were growing reports of frogs that were deformed—for example, missing a rear leg. More worrisome, herpetologists who were studying frog populations found that the frog numbers were dropping sharply—or the frogs had disappeared completely. By the year 1990, it was clear that frogs were in trouble all over the world.

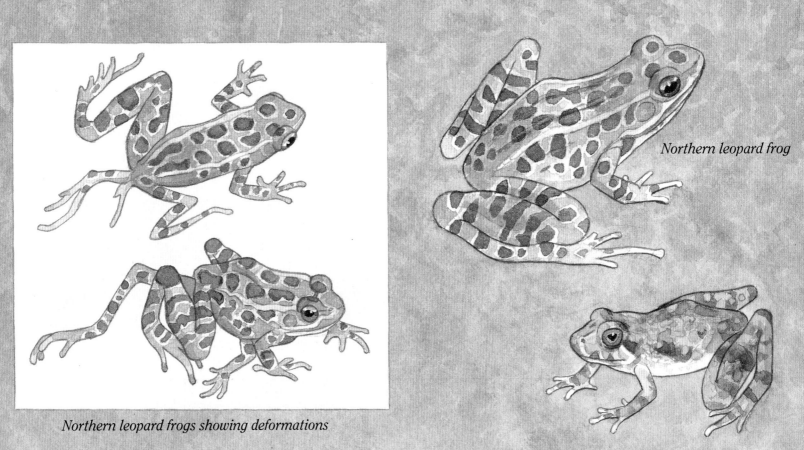

Northern leopard frogs showing deformations

Northern leopard frog

Northern cricket frog

Gastric-brooding frog

Golden toad

Harlequin frog

Tomato frog

The northern leopard frog was once common in Canada. Now it is scarce and missing from most of western Canada. The same is true of the northern cricket frog, gone from major parts of Midwestern states where it used to live. Worldwide, dozens of other species have become extinct. One of the most remarkable frogs—and greatest losses—is the gastric-brooding frog of Australia. This species had a unique way of raising young. Females swallowed fertilized eggs, then stopped eating for about six weeks, until little froglets developed inside their stomachs and hopped out of their mouths.

Soon after this amazing way of reproduction was discovered, these rain forest frogs disappeared. None have been seen since 1980. A cloud forest species, the golden toad, once lived in great numbers in part of Costa Rica's Monteverde Cloud Forest Reserve. None have been seen since 1989.

Why are frogs in trouble? In most instances, frogs (and salamanders) have dwindled in numbers or disappeared because their habitats have been destroyed. Forests are cut down, wetlands drained or filled in. Remaining ponds and other wetlands are sometimes polluted. Because many frogs spend part of their lives in water and part on land, they are exposed to pollution in both water and air.

Loss of habitat is the single greatest threat to frogs. But anurans are also vanishing in protected wilderness parks. In some places, the threat is other species that are released in wetlands. In California's Sierra Nevada Mountains, trout were stocked in lakes where no fish had lived before. Several kinds of frogs and salamanders were wiped out by the trout. (When trout are removed from mountain lakes, amphibian numbers increase.)

The warming of Earth's climate, caused largely by humans, also seems to harm frogs. Amphibians are sensitive to small changes in temperature and moisture in their environments. Another threat is the chytrid (kit-rid) fungus, which has killed frogs in all sorts of habitats. It causes a frog's skin to thicken and may block its ability to breathe through its skin. Chytrid has reduced frog numbers in 43 countries and 36 U.S. states.

Herpetologists are studying frogs all over the world, trying to learn more about the threats to their survival. They hope to find a way to protect frogs from the deadly chytrid fungus. Anurans have lived on Earth for at least 180 million years. They outlived the dinosaurs, mammoths, and many other extinct animals. Now frogs face new threats, mostly caused by humans. Only people can take the steps needed to stop the decline and disappearance of frogs.

Author's Note—A Life Full of Frogs

Many frogs and toads have leaped and hopped into my life. One early memory is the magical sound of spring peepers near my childhood home in the country south of Rochester, New York. Another memory is a sad one: my brother and I caught some small frogs, including toads, and put them in a "zoo"—an enclosure of wire mesh with a metal floor. The "zoo" was left in the sun. That day I learned that frogs and toads need shade and moisture to survive.

In those early years I also learned about a defense that a toad sometimes uses when you grab one and pick it up. It pees in your hand!

Later, as a wildlife photographer, I slowly stalked frogs and took close-up pictures. Often they sat still for their portraits. They lived in ponds and other wetlands of New York's Adirondack Mountains and had probably never seen a human before.

More adventures with frogs occurred when I became a father and took my kids out into nature. One June day we found hundreds of tadpoles in shallow puddles. The sun beat down on the water, and no rain was forecast. In just another day or two the puddles would be gone—and the tadpoles would die. We scooped up as many as we could and carried them to shady, deeper water where they had a good chance of becoming frogs.

A few years ago, I shoveled out many wheelbarrow-loads of soil and rocks, making a garden pond about twelve feet wide and fifteen feet long. Surrounded by moss-covered rocks and wetland plants, it looks like a wild, natural pond—both to people and to wildlife. Dragonflies visit and lay eggs. Months later, young adult dragonflies emerge from the pond. This summer, three bullfrogs and one green frog traveled overland from another wetland and made this little pond their home.

In a nearby swampy woods, spring peepers used to gather to mate each year. However, fallen dead leaves gradually changed to soil, causing low places to hold less water. After two years of drought, no peepers survived to mate and produce young. Once more I set to work with a shovel, deepening places so they would hold water long enough for peeper tadpoles to develop into adults. Then I drove to a pond where peepers were abundant in the spring. Wading in hip boots, I netted peeper tadpoles, then let them go in the little ponds I had dug.

Once again, a chorus of peepers announces spring to the families in my neighborhood.

Answer Key to Pages 16 and 17

Gray tree frog   *Canyon tree frog*   *Amazon horned frog*   *Red-eyed tree frog*

Vietnamese mossy frog   *Chinese microhylid*   *Soloman Island leaf frog*   *Ornate horned frog*

Spring peeper

More about Frogs and Their Conservation

A vital step in frog conservation is protecting their habitat—in your neighborhood, state, nation, and around the world. There are numerous groups whose main goal is preserving wildlife habitat. A few of these are

The Nature Conservancy, 4245 N. Fairfax Drive, Arlington, VA 22203; nature.org*
National Audubon Society, 225 Varick St., New York, NY 10014; audubon.org
Rainforest Action Network, 221 Pine St., Fifth Floor, San Francisco, CA 94104; ran.org
Wildlife Conservation Society, 2300 Southern Blvd., Bronx, NY 10460; wcs.org
World Wildlife Fund, 1250 24th St. NW, P.O. Box 97180, Washington, DC 20090; worldwildlife.org

For more information about frogs, their lives, and their conservation, visit these sites:
amphibiaweb.org
frogs.org
midwestfrogs.com
savethefrogs.com
And see this documentary film: Frogs: The Thin Green Line.

* Websites active at time of publication